Border States

What does it mean to settle somewhere? "Planting the fall bulbs yesterday," writes Jane Hoogestraat in Border States, "I thought as I often do / of what it means to settle here." Whether it's the South Dakota of family memory or a Missouri homeplace marked by seasonal rituals, Hoogestraat's poems are poems of place, never easy in their allegiances, always haunted by what was. When "The Battle Hymn of the Republic" and some Civil War re-enactors show up early in the book, for example, we are reminded that Missouri had stars on both flags and suffered violent internal conflicts that echoed the greater war beyond. And in a poem for Matthew Shepard, we learn to love the West as "the idea of a place where no one,/ knowing your story, feels at home." The poems for her parents in the book's last section are deeply moving--Keats's urn and Stevens' jar replaced by an heirloom wedding vase that leaves her "wishing I could remember, or even imagine / where the vase stood." In these poems, we hear accents we don't quite recognize, remember words we've forgotten how to say, find old hunting camps where fires still burn, and wear a camo shirt to fit in. "I wanted you to know everything at once," she tells us in "River Roads," "a landscape it took me months to learn." These are landscapes it takes months, years, lifetimes to learn, and Hoogestraat is our best guide.

—Ed Madden, Jr.
Nest and Signals

Border States

Jane Hoogestraat

Winner of the John Ciardi Prize for Poetry
Selected by Luis J. Rodriguez

BkMk Press
University of Missouri-Kansas City

BkMk Press
University of Missouri-Kansas City
5101 Rockhill Road
Kansas City, Missouri 64110
(816) 235-2558 (voice)
(816) 235-2611 (fax)
www.umkc.edu/bkmk

Cover Photo: "Courthouse Arches" by Peter Thody
Author Photo by Paula Moore
Book design: Marie Mayhugh, Michael Mayhugh
& Susan L. Schurman
Managing Editor: Ben Furnish
Associate Editor: Michelle Boisseau
Printer: McNaughton-Gunn

BkMk Press wishes to thank Marie Mayhugh, Derek Cowsert, Brittany Green, and
Megan Folken.

The John Ciardi Prize for Poetry wishes to thank Susan Cobin, Greg Field,
Lindsey Martin-Bowen, Linda Rodriguez, and Maryfrances Wagner.

Library of Congress Cataloging-in-Publication Data
Hoogestraat, Jane Susan, 1959-
[Poems. Selections]
Border states / Jane Hoogestraat.
pages cm
"Winner of the John Ciardi Prize for Poetry, Selected by Luis J. Rodriguez" -- Verso title
page.
 Summary: "These poems reflect on varied American themes such as diversity between
geographical locations, people, cultures, vernacular, rural life, folk music, history, and
the poet's search for identity and meaning in contemporary American life"-- Provided by
publisher.
 ISBN 978-1-886157-95-8 (pbk. : alk. paper)
1. U.S. states--Poetry. 2. American poetry. 3. National characteristics, American--Poet-
ry. 4. United States--Poetry. I. Title.
 PS3608.O57A6 2014
 811'.6--dc23
                    2014024142

This book is set in Rockwell and Garamond Pro.

Acknowledgments

Versions of several of these poems also appear in chapbooks: *Harvesting All Night* (Finishing Line—Winner of the Open Competition 2009) and *Winnowing Out Our Souls* (Foot Hills Press, 2007).

Grateful acknowledgment is also made to the following magazines in which many of these poems first appeared, sometimes in different form and under different titles.

Crab Orchard Review, "Gifts That Strangers Bring"

DoubleTake, "Driving through Kentucky"

Elder Mountain, "The Collector," "Hyacinth Boy," "To See Beyond Our Bourne,"

Fourth River, "Air Waves Over Iowa"

High Plains Literary Review, "Chicago Winter" and "Against the Urban Night"

Image, "Counting Winters" and "White River Dust"

Kansas Quarterly, "Crocuses"

Mars Hill Review, "A Hymn Heard through a Distant Window"

Midwestern Gothic, "At the Edge of a Time Zone," and "Not the People of God's Finest Hour"

Moon City Review, "Off I-29 in South Dakota" and "One Beautiful Storm, and Then Another"

North Dakota Quarterly, "Near Brooking, South Dakota" and "Morning Fields"

OzarksWatch, "Encountering the Militia at Wilson's Creek"

Poem, "River Roads," "Among the Benedictines," and "Last Class in Rhetoric"

Poetry, "Background Music"

Potomac Review, "Wind Turbines in Southern Minnesota"

Slant, "Harvesting All Night," and "Sica Hollow"

Southern Poetry Review, "Summer Darkness"

Southern Review, "Dark, Small Town Streets," "The Surprising Springs," "The Idea of Wyoming," "A Border State Celebrates the 4th of July," "Black Amethyst," "Listening to Faure," "A Letter to San Francisco," and "Near Red Lodge, Montana"

Tendril, "Balconies We Stood On" and "The Death of the Khan"

University of Chicago Magazine, "Abidance"

Yarrow, "What Prairie Flowers"

Yonder Mountain: An Anthology of Ozarks Poetry. Edited by Antony Priest. Fayetteville: University of Arkansas Press. "Béla Fleck Plays the Ozarks" and "Listening to Fauré"

Border States

II.

III.

IV.

Foreword

It was my honor to choose Jane Hoogestraat's *Border States* for the John Ciardi Prize for Poetry. These are poems with the spell binding power of the American Midwestern landscape, tapping into its emotional well, not just the physical beauty and expanse.

I fell deep into Hoogestraat's metaphors, the vivid imagery, the deft sleight of hand that brings magic to poetry. I'm familiar with the smells, dust and faces of these Border States, having lived fifteen years in Chicago and have given talks or readings in many of the places Hoogestraat brings to our heart's door.

The people, the soil, the tumultuous skies are unforgettable, as are these poems, and that's the most important aspect of language in verse—the way it makes you feel and think, a binary connection. This is how the sounds and sentiments get imprinted onto a soul.

Read and savor. The way great poems must be taken in, tasted or devoured, and then to return to them again and again—and get pulled into the magic each time.

—Luis J. Rodriguez

I

A Hymn Heard through a Distant Window

The darkness was Protestant that year, but not
with individual conscience, the hymn of the South,

or the priesthood of the believer. Haunted,
driving north, I watched the horizon gray

over Oklahoma, the rim of fires drifting down
from Manitoba. I stepped out hours later

to the first cold of September, a season's end.
The magnolias were already old those last evenings,

reflected in the watery light of summer rain.
But this spring, a hymn heard through

a distant window brought back the years
before: The places where crepe myrtle blooms

early and late, where almost every lamppost has a name
and shadows cross our days without erasing joy.

Gifts That Strangers Bring

Words I had forgotten how to say,
accents I had never heard,
the song about going home to Kansas
I listened to on a late-night talk show
and have searched for ever since,
not really hard enough to find.

The obscure book I left for a later reader.
Every face I've ever mistaken for another
I was, for an impossible moment, glad to see.

The black candlesticks she handed me that revealed
red translucent and blue shadows in the room
when I lit the first white candle of the season.
Every face and name that light recalled.

LEARNING TO LIVE IN THE UPLAND SOUTH

I've mowed the gladiola down, trimmed the barberry,
watered the yew. The walls in my house
are white, the wood polished, the glass dusted.

The season waits, still warm, though turning toward
mild winter the middle South. Not much.
Trees are in their autumn beauty, the cedar mulch

is dry. The neighbors have one pink flamingo, thank God
not nineteen, they keep having to retrieve
from other lawns. I still don't teach Sexton or Plath,

make jokes about poetry and gin, or laugh
with those who do. I know that tulips can be cold
but I've not seen them black. North across industrial yards

white temple churches rise, a neighborhood Falwell
once called home, school to his heart.
Driving back across his city this Sunday morning

I've proven what I needed to, remembering again
haunting lines, not often sung in our Battle Hymn:
I have read a fiery gospel writ in burnished rows of steel,

as ye deal with my condemners, so with you my grace shall deal.
We will be a while in this town winnowing out our souls.

Balconies We Stood On

Driving across the city this morning
over bridges fragile in the rain,
I thought of iron balconies surrounding
the places where we used to live, how we used
to lean over them talking the night away,

watching the light glisten on magnolias
in the courtyard below, watching the smoke
from our cigarettes rising toward the stars,
noticing the tangible that delivered us
from too much wordless thought.

And just past a gap in the guard rail,
twisted aluminum where the night before
a driver had missed a curve, I thought
of the night on the balcony you said
you wanted a mind so open it would

never close on anything again.
We were watching a storm, holding to the railing—
the metal vibrating like the pulse of a nerve
as the trees above us bent away,
the wind receded from us,

tearing boats loose from moorings downstream.
When even the touch of iron
disappeared beneath our fingers, you said
this is what it's like: the mind so open
in the center of the storm.

And when I passed the trees in bloom,
driving almost blind through the rain,
I thought of the last night we leaned
against the railing, in late August
when the crepe-myrtle blossoms were falling

to cover the asphalt in bright patches
that would fade before morning
like chalk drawings on the sidewalks
in Montmartre. You asked that night
about the point of poetry, and what to do

with pain. We talked until morning about how
the light makes patterns in the rain,
the paper on a cigarette burns in rings,
about how the stubborn mind looks for order,
looks for the railing that will hold.

Summer Darkness

Stepping that spring into rain with nothing
to protect the papers he carried rolled carelessly,
he paused, turning with a gaze beyond arrogance,
as though he meant to relinquish all caution,
never seek shelter in lighted doorways again
or speak another human word about danger.

Tonight fans rotate tediously, sirens announce
how late it has all become, the summer darkness
settles in, not less for coming later, breath
denser than winter and slower to arrive or leave,
and his face, voiceless, returns with a warning
from a corner in the mind that says only swerve.

A Border State Celebrates the Fourth of July

Bruce Springsteen's melody is playing in heavy bass
Muzak about our hometowns while a little blond boy stands
with his head slumped over the grocery cart in the line
behind me. I scrutinize his parents, wishing I could tell
who has the problem. *Cosmopolitan,* which I pick
up with no earthly intention of buying, well maybe,
has a feature on Kathleen Turner, who speaks,

an Eastern critic notes, in an accent known
to no identifiable ethnic group. I thought she was good
as V.I. Warshawski, Chicago accent, swagger.
Outside the first wisp of the moon appears
in a pale sky. In backyards, mauve and lilac
peonies bend burdened toward the green earth.
It's four days away from the Fourth of July in a postliterate

country, in a state settled by Anglo-Southerners and Prussians.
The clerk who knows my name tells me about a customer
who's always yelling at his wife—last week because she wanted
to buy a soda. From the back of the line, the scary-looking man
with a beard he hasn't trimmed in years, almost no teeth
but nevertheless clean overalls says in a bass
voice more gentle than I thought to hear,

No one should have to put up with that. I turn around,
nod, chagrined that I hadn't looked at him before.
In a cab on the way home from the grocery store,
the driver waits until we're almost at my place and says,
you're early tonight. I contemplate briefly my role
in this most peculiar version of postindustrial, postmodern,
non-Edenic-American culture, and fall for all of it again.

THE COLLECTOR

for Frank Vincent

So there really were rag-and-bone shops
with tattered Irish linen, scraps Baudelaire's
rag pickers traded in. So there really was
a heart, might be again, remnants.

New to this city, two decades gone,
I stumbled into an old flea market,
row after row of chicken wire cages,
canning jars full of childhood marbles,

didn't know what I was seeing: metal tins,
old kitchen implements, gasoline signs
wooden tools. Before *Antiques Road Show*,
pickers, there probably were treasures

or at least artifacts of a culture worth reading
had I taken home a jar to find spinning puries,
tigerseye, steelies, green ghosts,
paisley, *glaukos*, light on the olive trees

first green, then gray. Say there really was
a heart, know that again, guard
whatever made a student write
from Italy *we are the mist among the stones.*

ENCOUNTERING THE MILITIA AT WILSON'S CREEK

On a model of Gettysburg, the troops assemble
on a light board, forever replaying their formations,
the Union almost winning, later claiming the town
from its garrison in Springfield, a fact apparently not lost
on the Missouri State Guard, touring with their historian,
their white buses, the red hats of the unreconstructed South.

They are still hopelessly outnumbered, know that
it's a lost cause, but they are renegades who would *rather
break than bend*, and from reading the slogans on their shirts,
the places, I do believe they mean that. They inspire
fear, not heritage, with their flags, their Confederate
money handed out like so many idle souvenirs.

Because I want to understand, I take our folk historian
to Fort 5 in Springfield, wondering how a border town
amassed such a collection of forts, of war memorabilia,
medals it is now illegal to wear. The owner directs
us to a history of the Civil War in Springfield, not one
he keeps in stock, almost surprised that we have asked.

Someday I will inquire what all these armaments mean
in a region where they still sing "Onward Christian Soldiers,"
all five stanzas considered too militant elsewhere, where
"The Battle Hymn of the Republic," once a northern Yankee
Hymn, underwrites more than one Southern school's song,
whose hymns of war are these, whose hymns?

BÉLA FLECK AND THE FLECKTONES PLAY THE OZARKS

Yes, the banjo can hit the ironic,
scale the world's notes, which we would have known

had we tried earlier to learn the real music of the place
where we live, tried a little. Can a banjo, also, carry

the craggy resources of a place, a violent area,
where outside the garrison town, there was no law,

a bitter place that simmers in its stories,
needs its banjo, fiddle, if you will, to call the riffs,

the dances, to name the stories . . . to lighten and to lift,
to keep the score, to remember what it cannot heal?

The Hyacinth Boy

Just four, he kneels by hyacinths, speaking quietly
words I cannot understand, walks to the next bed,
kneels again. He helps me weed until I tell him

no, that's the crepe myrtle, it's not dead. Too soon
he will learn not to show fondness for flowers,
or maybe it's the yard he likes. How to treat this child

with enough gentleness, help him grow into a love
for color, design, for whatever he might choose.
His father in prison, this boy expelled from preschool.

Is he old enough, I ask, to be told simply to stop
calling names. His grandmother shakes her head,
says a stone starts small but will grow

if not addressed, and she has seen that anger start in him
hardening his young days. He may never have
words for what he needs. I imagine him on a college green

somewhere, learning a little Eliot, charming a friend
with his knowledge. Not impossible . . . . Already this spring
when there is no way to treat this child with enough gentleness.

NOT THE PEOPLE OF GOD'S FINEST HOUR

Uninvited, not particularly welcome at evening Mass,
one of the almost homeless brings two younger men,
clearly homeless, troubled, and they fence me in.
I could slip out the side, sit elsewhere, leave,
and I consider that, before I smile, ask if they have been
through a service before, explain the Prayer Book.

Before the Rite I Eucharist (long), one has heard enough,
while the other, reeking softly of smoke
fidgets, then folds his head on the rail, dozes
until we begin the Lord's Prayer
which he probably knows from mandatory recovery
and for a minute he actually does belong here.

There are degrees of disaffection, most clear to the disaffected.
Even here, in this rag-tag service, where heaven help us,
I am the one, who after the priest, appears to know the service—
what cadence to use in reading the creed (used on feast days),
which the homeless did read earlier, wrecking the rhythm,
the priest having to speak louder to restore some order.

Wherever they land tonight—an apartment called "little Iraq,"
a meth nexus known as "the Hollow," a camp near the tracks,
or a shelter named "Rare Breed," whose inhabitants I've passed,
avoiding their eyes, when I enter the city's best restaurant, "Flame"—
wherever they land, may they remember, not fear,
the priestly blessing, the one prayer we all had to learn.

The Surprising Springs

for my sister

I used to miss the day each year the city breaks
blossoms, only days later knowing the season,
how it changes in our favor. I watch for it now
as the day in March when the dogwoods open
more perfectly than a design painted on china
or black glass, ever darkening spring skies.

This season shrubs flowered early in Lent
by the Episcopal church, Miracle Gro, no doubt,
from the Garden Guild, again. The cherry trees
seemed blanched, except near dusk when the Don't Walk sign
caught a corner of a tree and turned it neon red.
Only the forsythia seemed not to blink, instantly yellow.

I'll remember this one as the year it snowed
in April, the start of your third year healthy,
your children two years older, our parents hale,
a family that learned, and not too late, that forgiveness
and humor are gifts finer than the first crocus of the year,
all the gardens, and their surprising springs.

Listening to Fauré

This morning the darkest green, the coldest spring
fell away before a sunlit clearing where a cardinal
and a jay teased a squirrel. Later an overcast sky held
until we were inside, purple irises withstood the storm.
When in the night you turn to cross another year,
think of this music, how it will not cease
returning the same lines, richer year by year
like those late green thunderstorms we've watched nights
from the living room. We keep our candles lit
long after midnight, after the sirens,
in the region of what little peace there is.

By June when the first fireflies are out, a neighbor
will light four corner candles for guests to play croquet
far into night. Others will watch from a porch swing.
Another visiting poet has written to say *you live
in very paradise there*, where the evening light
falls less eerily than the fireflies after they have flared,
too suddenly green, gone. Enough evenings like that,
we won't curse the cold spring storms that leave this town
too green, or think instead of all that we were spared.

Background Music

What Satie must have heard in the interval
when light was changing, a bird, one note short,
or a trill that repeated, left unresolved
the moment it happened in the century.

How much he must have distrusted performance,
known no one would play the same three-note sequence
eighty-seven times. He taught us to imagine
that score, and he brought everything to it,

reached backward to the medieval chant through Brahms
to the folly of pure entertainment, the Parisian street,
the impoverished room he lived in, *undistinguished waltzes
of a jaded dandy*, he said once. Ten years in silence.

The cafés where he played the notes that became
furniture, where background music started, remain still
to be imagined, music through the veil of that history
played over and over, as soothing and unfinished,

the music of flowers that hold rain effortlessly,
of simple rooms with polished floors, of the glance
that missing nothing does not turn away, of the first
step on the landing and the calm, then, in the heart.

River Roads

That afternoon we walked above the river
I wanted you to know everything at once,
a landscape it took me months to learn,
how the light touches a bridge silver
miles away, the streams that lead
into the Missouri below—Hart, Apple Creek,
and the roads that hide along the river,
how one tree in the ravine will turn red soon,
others a paler shade of green to seem
for one fall day as they do in spring,
and the light here, how it is never the same.

How haze hangs over the river roads
even into spring when the fog lifts
quiet laughter in the morning air,
something breaking free, the world for once
coming clean, even then a haze will veil
the currents of the river, lace the road,
and so driving there in early spring
or late summer means following a voice
both soothing and disturbing, although softer
than despair, say as in winter when from rooms
above the city you don't know if people
passing below are speaking or only
following their own white breath.

Off I-29 in South Dakota

She was drinking tea, not dressed for weather,
smoking, counting loose change to collect
enough for a meal. And writing. In midwinter
at a truck stop, the rigs with their thunder
but far from any town. How to measure
that memory, ask for a late blessing?

I will never know her story, she the blessing,
the haunting way her face pale with weather
reminds me of others' isolation. That measure
balancing small complaints, as in the collect
to make no peace with oppression, the thunder
silenced in sub-zero glare, years ago, in winter.

To be so alone in light clothes in winter
frightens me, solitude with no blessing,
the endless interstate, the blizzard, no thunder
to prepare the heart for calmer weather.
The gesture of how words and change collect,
provide the hours with their own measure.

I trust those earliest of memories, measure
of a child paying attention, in a long winter
over a half-eaten plate, sorting images to collect
the stories, traveling that land. With a blessing
if not of peace then of clarity, weather
of compassion. What remains after the thunder.

In summer, heat lightning without thunder
cracks open miles of landscape, to measure
the harsh, extreme swings of climate, weather
that marks this country desolate. Less so in winter
when austerity might emerge as a blessing,
a sky acute in its pink cold, an image to collect.

Whether she rode away, went home to collect
more clothes or left later, after the thunder,
set off older, secure in her search for a blessing,
a kinder version of herself, a way to measure
the distance between the drifter she was that winter
and the surer self emerging from such weather. . . .

How do we measure distance, remember the collect
in mid-winter, *to contend against evil*, thunder,
and odd weather, before the impossible blessing?

II

Among the Benedictines

Cold mornings now the whisper of spruce
disappears, haze veils the river, bells
toll the call to work or prayer, hours
Benedict gave the world in a dark century.

Under that sky, more than any other,
cold, clear, almost breathable stars
vaporized toward words, warmed the void
of a northern night, probably always will.

No one owns this, the sisters said, *no one knows.*
The light we have claimed does not belong
to us alone, nor any grace we have denied.
But they said little else, beyond the ironies

they vowed to live through, on the very edge
of sacred ground, they would not speak of consolation,
until that silence froze the road to glass,
all contrast gone, lashed the sky white, silver ice

until the scraps of paper I lived by seemed torn,
any road once worth taking home obscured,
snow drifting in from the west as I stood watching
from the room with windows on winter.

But more gift than betrayal in memory now.
White noise, almost as real as the hills
around the bell tower, always as distant,
hills backlit then by white light

the other side of the altar candle's flame,
a sky that burned under a bright void
taught me to travel more cautiously, the years
that made everything else possible.

Think of the first snow arriving, as it will
later tonight, falling for hours to reach us
with a sound more subtle than the sirens
we have slept through, to be the sound

that wakes us like a death chill at night,
when the mind walks the edge of a cold field
in the fear that slips by every filter,
before melting like snow against glass.

Among the Cistercians

I.

Driving in Ozarks gravel past a buggy,
past a white horse in the field, past CR something's
driveway after the NPR signal goes, then the cell,
after I decide to be lost for good

Douglas County appears, haven to meth labs,
Amish beards, Cistercian monks, the highest
unsolved murder rate in a single county,
and for three days my sorry nondevout self.

Visiting six years ago, I was dying young, chemo
setting blood on fire, a match lit to run the circuits,
my gray wig lifting away in the wind, skin the color
of sick winter sun. A less clever penitent then.

The frankincense I had forgotten, didn't notice
how the wand for incense looks vaguely
pharmaceutical, a cure perhaps to silence
self-importance, the troubled heart's devices.

II.

This morning I learned that wisdom is female
having arrived accidentally in the week
of Ordinary Time that also marks the Feast
of the Assumption, dear to Cistercians,

when extra Psalms are read at Vigils and at (3:30 A.M.),
a letter from Pope Pius II quoting the church fathers,
early and fine weavers of Mary's strange fiction
in a discourse so wild that eighteen hundred

years later a father stamped it authoritative.
Show some respect. Also daughters are mentioned
quite often in the Psalms, even a Queen of Heaven.
And what the church fathers termed *apathia*

only marks a beginning, the soul gleaming
like a golden cylinder when held to light,
here, there, intertwined with other lives,
rooms where frankincense burns, or love.

III.

But driving back, leaving the cloistered hours,
can be tricky, too, past Dawt Mill, the turnoff
to Romance (Missouri), knowing there are
colonies in these woods, others holding apart,

makers of organic peanut butter (nudists),
Primitive Baptists, First Churches of God
(Pentecostal), old hunting camps where fires
still burn, a reported gathering of the Klan.

So I carry a camo shirt in the car, have been called
(with affection) a good old girl for wearing it,
also in a size too large an orange hunting vest
implying a round of ammo, a shotgun in the trunk

and find, for the most part, a gentle people
cautious with strangers, my accent shielding me,
not suggesting I have spent half a lifetime here
haunted by how much can be hidden.

III.

Black Amethyst

Look for the phoenix, the phalanx, the reverse peacock
and wild-rose pattern, for elegant Depression-era glass
from Paden City, West Virginia, from a time before.
Look only for etched black, an ornate art nouveau design.
Brush the dust away, turn what you have found until
the black gloss, shining like ore, reveals another color
rare as the early morning of an easy departure. Paler
than cobalt, smoked ruby red, black amethyst must surely be
one of the thousand or so wonders we are given.
Hold carefully in your hands all you will know from a time
never yours. Try, as you think of the arts of a private life,
to remember in what accent and to whom you might ask:
Here, would you like this one? One afternoon many years ago
I came upon this one last, and though it wasn't very expensive,
finding it brought me joy in a dark time.

At the Edge of a Time Zone

Not the midnight sun exactly, or endless summer,
just that extra hour holding steady, western
horizon stable, as though shadows won't lengthen
when in August you can outrun the night
or feel as though you do, latitude in your favor,

North of Sioux City, the sky widens into South Dakota,
turn west and you will think you could see all the way
to Wyoming, and if you drive long enough you will,
crossing the Missouri River, the bluffs gentle,
then the grasslands, the turnoffs for reservations.

As dusk approaches, you may pass a stone house,
long deserted, a star carved over the door, a small pond,
wind stirring over it even now, forming a second thought,
a space you will carry within your speech,
your soul stirred by these great expanses.

NEAR BROOKINGS, SOUTH DAKOTA

Camping that night on family land
I heard someone walk away
over late September grasses
and stubble fields, without need
of a light. The step of deer
through harvested corn,
or the rustle of partridge
flying low over the grasses,
or the wind in a stray cottonwood,
these were not what I heard.
I turned the lantern down
not calling out. Someone who knew the land,
who could walk to the edge of the prairie
on a night when darkness seemed
not so much above as circular
was walking there.

I noticed the stars then,
they were as near to each other
as our minds must have been,
and as distant. In this country,
when someone who's been near
begins to leave, it's better not to turn,
wave them away.
This is reticence born not of fear
but the knowledge that some
who know the land
well prefer to walk the edges alone.

MORNING FIELDS

Flax like a river—that blue that fluid—
weaves the morning fields, a morning
come to the mind, some shared arrival.

The color of coolness, early summer,
the flash of a teal wing as it leaves
or loops slowly back, gliding now

with wings folded through air, water.
A rapid flicker, gone when I speak
to startle it, gone when I turn away

toward what the imagination holds.
Somewhere the flax flows through
its short June season, dark trees float

on the horizon, marking the mirage
of a lake that even from this distance
I might have been startled into seeing again.

Wind Turbines, Minnesota

I'd seen them from the other side of the border,
but coming across them over the green hills,
they seemed both too large and so small against the sky,

and one not working, a bent wing on its third
propeller, if that is what they are called. Wind towers
lined up as though to catch the best currents,

visible twenty miles from land so flat
you can see the curve of Earth on the horizon,
how it tips away a little at the end.

Rilke says that angels aren't interested in our view
of the cosmos, which they have mostly seen before:
they like to hear the little stories of our ordinary hours,

so an angel might like to hear about the broken wing
on the wind tower, how it seemed momentarily sad,
like one who couldn't fly, a small creature struggling.

Our response was the human, merely, *oh, that's too bad*
though unlike a bird's wing, someone will be able to fix it,
studying the storehouses of wind to find out how.

DARK, SMALL TOWN STREETS

Summers, elms would arch whole blocks
beneath a canopy that twenty years
into the neighborhood closed over,
branches above the widest street
denser season by season, protecting
white wood houses painted, stable
with discipline long outgrown its use.

Around every corner still the sprinkler
sweeps its perfect arc, before turning
with a click to start the same round
over, until the click stops seeming trivial
and becomes a metronome of anger,
fear or pulse, tediously whispering
summer's haunting refrain.

Or perhaps the interruptions
make us want the older music back again,
whatever we hear behind what soothes
and disconcerts—the sound of a ball
returned from the center of the strings,
the fan lifting a single page from a desk
and setting it down in another summer.

Were there no answers there
beyond what every lighted house
held and the elms we almost shared,
all sufficient for the evening ritual
of talking while the darkness fell
toward shadows where great trees once were,
green lawns, so much we held in common.

CHICAGO WINTER

The *Times* this morning features a chart for light
viewed through cathedral windows, another for tracing
a labyrinth on a stone floor that makes sense
for anyone who starts to find a way through.
Every traveler learns eventually how the night sky
of a city, especially from the air, speaks of home.

We are always asking how we are to make
our lives, moving through the stark winter on nerve,
waking the dark hours where the labyrinthine roots
of our pasts rise to the edges of our voices,
asking for a consoling story, hoping to be happy
when we leave. It is that simple.

It is Sunday afternoon and snowing.
The afternoon trumpets are muted and clear
in the better brunch music of the early seventeenth century
when language was changing its world. The sky is cold
and polished and not what we need.

We are talking politely of what we do not care about
as a way of learning a different aesthetic, as a way
of starting home, away from this formal quality called,
not inappropriately, being at a loss.

A Brief History of Spartan Rooms

I thought it must be like this in a monastery where you had
company and sympathy but your thoughts were your own.
—Jeanette Winterson

The lure of simplicity, rooms in university clubs
spartan dorm rooms, rooms where thinking
might actually take place, monasteries,
shore cabins with sand everywhere authentic.

In the eighties, still signs on Chicago's Southside
for residential hotels, whose décor echoed Hopper,
my own graduate room in a converted hotel
an odd flake of snow drifting through.

So that even my house recreates the 1930s,
includes the lantern my mother did her work
by that decade. She bears no nostalgia for that time,
or the return of cotton some years ago, the iron.

I've taken colors from *A Room in Brooklyn*—
a tablecloth the color of brick dust echoing
a building visible in three windows, sills dark amber,
and in a square of light, a rocking chair, a woman reading.

Against the Urban Night

for Billy Clem

Remember from routes tangled now the precise
slant of light on the pavement, acres of power
generators for probably seven states, powder-blue
petroleum tanks, flares, and all the turns that might
have gone the other way. Because we have two stories
both true, will it help if we remember this road?

An hour later, wooded country begins to appear,
late transformation marked at night by darker air,
suddenly still. Fewer lights on the side of the road
signal private victories won against public darkness,
places we once lived, warily though not in despair.

PROVINCETOWN HARBOR

Modernist painters settled for obscurity here
rather than leave, transformed unheated coal bins
to studios. The blue they saw still coats

the harbor indigo near dusk, changing before our eyes,
or must our eyes adjust, color a gift of consciousness
light itself shifting what it dreams?

Light the very place itself dreams, not just the painter,
cyclists on the shore, a pair casting for blue fish,
an offshore trawler guarding its treasure.

Under a slate sky, Moffett's fishermen trudge
the coast past horse-drawn wagons, ploughs,
the travail of the Portuguese, winter. His innovation

the shadowed world, muted history, snow falling on water
and in a corner, a green basket filled with sea plums.

Driving through Kentucky

I'm stuck on a road called the Mountain Parkway
behind coal trucks from truck mines, afraid
to even think about turning on the radio.

Already in West Virginia my friend had to order
for me, using a range I've never heard,
a slow accent of strip towns and gaps and hollows,

of sulfur burning at night, of people I've feared
and despaired of. *Don't talk,*
Don't get out of the truck, and don't talk.

East of here, night still falls on the Cumberland.
On roads cut through limestone, coal veins grow
less visible as darkness fills the gaps,

rises from the valleys to where the daylight
lingers, and perhaps a candle or lamp is lit
when Charleston factory lights have burned for hours.

What has been lost from the core of these mountains,
neither Jesus nor the Klan nor all the snake charmers
can bring back. Old country does not grow young again

not now, and not in the fierce silence of the Ozarks
settled later, days, years from here. As if the speech
we listen hardest to is not the speech that's strange,
as if we don't wish most of all to be understood.

Air Waves Over Iowa

The early settlers weren't thinking of the view
from the air, how the surveying lines
would hold, a quarter section marking
a house squared by a trimmed lawn,
a small flower garden visible from the road.

When radio was new, Adorno noted
an ideal where farmers in Iowa might listen
to a Boston symphony. He said it couldn't work,
though some listening did go on, especially in the fall,
while the late crickets chirped in the asters outside.

He also said that Germans had put classical music
to the wrong instrumental uses, and he worried
about the atomization of music, predicting
the devices that separate us even further,
a music without history, industrial jazz.

But back to radio music. Take a Schubert symphony
heard for the first time—a hymn, a Mass, lieder,
pantheism creeping in, a little gathering together
to ask a blessing, where one might hear a melody
in the dark sounds, a speaking of light near morning.

THE IDEA OF WYOMING

for Matthew Shepard

The snow falls now in Casper and Laramie,
large early season flakes, no covering fine enough
for you, who should have been okay in a landscape
that flattens accents, makes travelers quiet,
cowboys wellmannered, descendents
of those who survived here proud.

Nothing in the landscape, burning sage,
the winter wind, the howl of the coyote,
summer's searing light, homesteaders who
starved here, the river bottomland already
taken when the area opened for settlement,
nothing in this wind-driven fault-dry basin

of land was ever designed to be cruel.
Not to you, not to the internees at Heart Mountain
during the war, not to the Arapaho, the Cheyenne,
the Czech, the Slovak. No one is proud now.
Imagine candles burning, in every ranch house,
every small town, every city, every Western tavern

with its horns above the mirror, its grizzly bear,
its straight shooters, the thwack
of the cue ball, the swish of rag on a long bar—
Imagine a culture that harvests together, and herds
across boundaries, where stories travel far into night.
Remember how the night sounds when the moon rises

over an endless road winding through alkali flats
and sage, with only antelope and the kindness
of drivers, of those who love this land and might have
loved you, who will now have to love the West
in new ways, in the idea of a place where no one,
knowing your story, feels at home.

IV.

LAST CLASS IN RHETORIC

for my father

After years of teaching Cicero
and Quintilian, memory and invention,
he writes, *On the retirement, there is no remorse,*
nor do I anticipate there will be any.

Who now understands why Aristotle
privileged ethos, who we listen to, why?
Does he, who *has been doing a little pruning*
on the trees on the east end of the south row?

Always the diffident voice of the scholar
who does not quite trust his own work—
Many birds were back. More robins, more red wings,
one pair of mallard ducks in full color,
and a variety of unidentified warblers.

May I remember kindness this precise, the care
he takes to describe a world, always hear this range,
know the role his voice must play in mine.

One Beautiful Storm, and Then Another

Eighty years my father lived on this land
and never saw before this ice light, stalks
of switchgrass frozen, dead corn fields
glimmering with a little of what heaven
must be like, Russian olive trees, ash,
poplar, bent but not broken, outlined
against a post-solstice sky, his daughters,
granddaughters, walking across the farm,
climbing up the deer stand for the view.

This morning, Frost's twig touched a corner
of my face. I brushed it away, annoyed,
and understood a little more of the poem
I've read for years, then hacked away again
at the isinglass of the car windows, mourned
the dogwood, checked on the river birches,
thought without nostalgia of kerosene lines,
vacant traffic signals, the whole gray world
of fatigue and cold and minor meltdowns.

The immigrants endured far worse, of course,
and left no art behind about the endless winter,
the one-room dugouts. I wonder what they talked
about those seasons, what they hoped for.
My great-grandfather looked out one day,
saw the railroad crew in a distance, walked over
and asked for a job. He would laugh, I think,
to know the price of David Plowden's *Golden Valley,
North Dakota,* a picture of an elevator, train tracks

hanging on the warm wall of my house. A gift
from Yale, or rather from a friend there, who
found it for me after I'd switched seats
with her at dinner, she already having gotten
into it with a priest over too much red wine,
some talk about White Russians and socialists
of all things. That grandfather had his views
as well about the Bolsheviks, the peasants,
the Bruderhof, the old country he so missed.

In one tradition, one should not die before
having seen a thousand wonders. How to count?
One wonder a day? A counting through years?
A farm with two trees on it when he bought it,
now has thousands, an owner to pay attention,
no, not that great grandfather, the father who tilled
these trees, who lived to see the rarest of ice storms,
who once said, *we may not be here in another
hundred years, but these grasses will be, these trees.*

HARVESTING ALL NIGHT

Twenty years ago, my father stops
in the small farm town where he was a boy
to watch his nephews, already men, play softball.
The long arc of a ball hit toward the far corner

leaves the light behind for a long sigh.
He told us later he wanted to stay that night.
When the harvest is late, the ground too muddy,
the players will wait until the earth freezes, then harvest

all night, the sodium lights of expensive combines
eerie as UFOs on the horizon, ringed by frost stars.
A family cemetery dated 1949 holds now the second
generation after the immigrants, and a few small graves

from the third. It will all last another generation or two,
be tended, that cemetery, the games in the park.
Dvořák visiting in Iowa caught it once,
as it retreated from him, a country that could

not be his, although he called it a new world, and brave.
His largo captures all he would know
of native melody, the indigenous music of the plains
that will outlive everything we're losing, everything we are.

The Death of the Khan

So much remains forever unexplained
of the night the horsemen arrived,
their hair frozen black behind them,
men who rode beyond words for returning
or son or daughter or home, who stopped
in a village on the edge of Germany,
helping first from his horse the khan
who would not live the night. Before morning
his lifeless body would be lashed to his horse,
most of the riders and all of the horses gone,
riding back along a route of blackened villages
they'd not return to plunder again.

The riders had no words for what
had driven them westward toward a sea
they could not have known was there,
had few words for the only knowledge
stronger than the fire they rode with,
the only certainty that would have stopped them:
that a khan could not be buried or chosen
away from his own country.

So much remains forever unexplained
about the riders for whom the hoard did not
return, who would never ride through burning
villages again, whose story would never
make sense in any language, about the women in the village
who had no names for the strangers,
but who would tell stories of children
since that night born with their dark eyes.

ABIDANCE

My father and his brothers hunt pheasants
through a fine October day, keeping one row of corn,
golden stubble, between them, sweeping the fields

of the homesteaders. It is 1946, the country
is at peace, and a minister from Princeton takes
the train to their South Dakota farms

to listen to their speech, Low German,
a Dutch inflection, the quiet mark of allegiance
to the low countries, now that the borders

are no longer terrible. When the evening light
becomes the fast-falling night, the time
of long shadows, he asks for a farmhouse,

a phone, and because something is abiding
in those fields he has not seen, calls the city
to say that he has been unavoidably detained.

SICA HOLLOW

for my nieces

Indian ginger, sharp-scented as curry,
grows there above underground springs
that creak at night from decay,
so that early visitors confusing mineral
with spirit named it *bad hollow*,
spoke of the light of spirits, a glow.

The tribes came here for medicine.
Even this sweltering August, strange
breezes cool the currents of air, water.
The trails take you out to knolls, tallgrass prairie where once a glacier
cut a soul's gateway to another world.

Indian ginger had other names: snakeroot, heart root.
It cured fevers in the spring. Its leaves could be
wrapped as a poultice. Powdered for snuff, it healed
aching heads and eyes, like oil from the camphor daisy
rubbed on a forehead to soothe what's strange.
It was best when ground for tea, reassuring and bitter.

Year after year, your mother was fascinated, returning
to this place, like an almost-real ghost story,
a spell to take away . . . For you, there,
memory will be antidote, will be medicine.
In that magical place you can pick ginger,
learn about care, cure, learning to take care.

COUNTING WINTERS

for my parents

From the end of September, you write of the winds,
the view that runs the ridge line from Nicollet Tower,
and I remember how terrible recent history seems there,
the lakes of childhood, the native grasslands,

this favorite campsite of roaming Dakota bands.
The Trail of Spirits winds toward Sica Hollow,
though the moss on the creek stones stays too green,
phosphorescent, almost eerie, until the ice whitens even that.

Traveling this season from north to south, I saw autumn twice,
as once friends traveling back and forth from Australia
gave their young son three years of a world without winter.
The color flames again and again this season, the synapses

of memory. I think of you, driving in uncertain times
to watch a season turning. How proud your joy makes me.
No thieves of time here, no sacred chants in this place
where in any season travelers will simply walk, always

leave before the light shading the springs goes black,
while the rim of the prairie holds the fine blue halo
of what we will forever, now, be driving toward.

What Prairie Flowers

for my mother

My mother saved for me her mother's wedding vase
heavy at the base, ringed there and near the rim
with years of tap-water rust, part of the glass now
beyond any hope of scouring. It's the oldest thing I own,
knowing a family quirk will also stop with me,
a certain startled look, an unremembered tick.
This morning I heard the neighbor's wind chimes
like a breeze through farm windows in the early cold.
I woke wishing I could remember, or even imagine,
where the vase stood, what prairie flowers grew
long-stemmed enough to reach the base
and if the rust came because she filled
the vase to the line each time or forgot once,
until the flowers dried on their stems.

To See Beyond Our Bourn

> *It is a flaw*
> *in happiness to see beyond our bourn,—*
> *It forces us in summer skies to mourn,*
> *It spoils the singing of the Nightingale.*

—Keats, *Epistle to John Hamilton Reynolds*

Planting the fall bulbs yesterday, I thought as I often do
of what it means to settle here, to plan ahead for spring
hyacinths, worry whether autumn crocuses will appear,
notice which asters are thriving just now, October Skiesand Wood
land Way. Under the harvest moon, low and full
in the western sky this week, sadness turns to gentleness.

To plant perennials is a gamble on the future self that
will care come spring what it had the forethought to do,
or care that others passing be cheered, as years ago
on Harper Street near the university a small front lawn filled
each summer with row upon row of gladioli. Twenty years gone,
off-season, they brighten the mind on an ordinary evening.

I was worrying about what to say to my students,
or help them learn to say, and planning to confess
I wondered which flowers would stay for extra seasons
when I'm no longer here to tend them, afraid planting
was some marker of the solitary. But now I've reversed myself,
not the sole arbiter of what matters, not the arbiter at all.

CROCUSES

DeQuincey remembered all his life
a pathos he could not articulate,
noticing by his second birthday
crocuses returning, a sense of time
learned too early, a mind that saw
too much and remembered more, haunted
by images others learned to forget.
The earliest crocus was more gentle
than the recurring year it marked,
of all images the most dreamlike,
memory of a world before words,
a world before imagination
became opium and time regret.
Already, in the fragile crocus,
a world of signs, of all returning.

WHITE RIVER DUST

The gateway to Pine Ridge is through the Badlands.
There I first heard the roar of silence, saw loss
pressed in stone layers, knew the despair of distance.

On the edge of Wounded Knee, I bought from a tribal
stand a necklace of malachite, prairie agate, a turtle
for bravery on the Turtle Island. Also two dream

catchers. An eagle feather woven with Lakota colors.
In addition, a circle woven in blue sky beads, buffalo horn,
for a strong woman. More than trinkets, less than talisman.

Not knowing how much I would need them,
not knowing how tough I would have to be
or in a few short months how very wrong.

The sweet grass fragrance of confidence is gone
for this season, not even winter sage would help.
In these winds, I might as well be there, the heart

wintering out in a tar-paper shack, white river dust
in the throat, the alkali taste of too much pride
swallowed too late, the bitter herb that will not heal,
the cedar berries drying into ghost beads.

POEM FOR THE NEW YEAR

Snow coats the Japanese stone lantern,
the prayer garden closed for the season.

Conversation drifts around a story too painful
for a friend to tell, her eyes explaining.

The story sinks in the soul like a stone,
pulling downward to where dark stars are born.

Perhaps a god has withdrawn, remains only
present with us again in certain music.

This afternoon I watched a finch
flit unaware within the winter hedge,

growing spare now yet a refuge,
an order for the turning year.

In the Japanese Garden

The morning directs us here
to an obelisk of flat fieldstones
compiled with care,
purple fountain grass
color of the wind
bowing as if blessing
the silver reflecting bowl,
empty before the future
placeholder of dreams.
When the tea ceremony ends
rewrap the bread
burn the spirit paper,
the candles of the fall
become kites in spring
and plum blossoms return.
Tell me again how exactly
we might have expected
any of this would happen?

A Letter to San Francisco

That year the gladioli bloomed late, variegated
crimson, scarlet, a quick flash of tangerine,
weighed down by the season, held by the heat.

Calling from the west, you asked weekly *were they
in flower yet?*, half afraid, I know,
that I had simply mowed them over, or left

them unattended to the season. Later
we picked and cut a stalk intent
on bending toward the ground, though twice

we twined it through the chain link fence
we share with nongardening neighbors.
Placing it in a black glass vase

your uncle helped us find, I understood
a little more of how fragile this world is,
how fine. He who asked *at what price life?*

and lived to the end in his beloved neighborhood
with his beloved, in a city with arboretums.
May his city bloom late this year also,

and may the fragile flowers on the shore
off Point Lobos catch, more than in a glass
spun darkly, some hint of a life as fine.

Near Red Lodge, Montana

Are even the field stones charred, the rugged sienna clay
on the road, the white rocks along the creek bed,
are they darkened like snow in a late urban winter?
Can a part of the past be torched, just like that,
by a lightning strike that has you hanging up the phone
on a year, a summer, on the green fields leading in?

Here's how it happened. Days earlier, near East Rosebud,
in isolated country behind Shepard Mountain
a lightning fork caught a tree, a patch of needles,
smoldered for days in its remoteness, then started
back drafting and blew, a fire that funneled the ravines,
jumped the smaller creeks, took out the grassy plains.

The sweet grasses lost in that fire, alfalfa, short grass,
buffalo, the trees, juniper, lodge pole, spruce, willow,
become only some residual sifting down from time to time,
ash of memory, dust of trivia, the unlabeled pictures
of the year . . . to whom was this year lost? Fire crews
will tell you they train to recognize what they can't save.

And here's how it comes back, when it does, new growth
from scorched earth. The fireweed spreads its roots,
then paintbrush or crocus. Spring snow cover melts away
over the first juniper seedlings, a start of mountain ash.
Lichen returns to a blackened trunk, spreads to the fragile base
of a lodgepole pine that has needed fire to seed.

Far from human fear or desire, the water rinses a little soot
from the edges of a still-charred rock, the kind a hiker
might pluck, polish like a talisman to carry home and hand
over, shyly, stupid and late, another one for your collection,
maybe for those rock gardens you've been designing,
dreaming of, from a little part of the world you used to know.

Jane Hoogestraat teaches at Missouri State University in Springfield. Her work has appeared in *Southern Review, Image, Crab Orchard Review*, and elsewhere, and she has published two chapbooks. An editor with *Moon City Review*, she also coedited the book *Time, Memory and the Verbal Arts: Essays on the Thought of Walter Ong*. She was educated at the University of Chicago and Baylor University. *Border States* is her first full-length poetry collection.

Winners of the John Ciardi Prize for Poetry

Border States by Jane Hoogestraat, selected by Luis J. Rodriguez

Beauty Mark by Suzanne Cleary, selected by Kevin Prufer

Secret Wounds by Richard M. Berlin, selected by Gary Young

Mapmaking by Megan Harlan, selected by Sidney Wade

The Tongue of War by Tony Barnstone, selected by B. H. Fairchild

Black Tupelo Country by Doug Ramspeck, selected by Leslie Adrienne Miller

Airs & Voices by Paula Bonnell, selected by Mark Jarman

Wayne's College of Beauty by David Swanger, selected by Colleen J. McElroy

The Portable Famine by Rane Arroyo, selected by Robin Becker

Fence Line by Curtis Bauer, selected by Christopher Buckley

Escape Artist by Terry Blackhawk, selected by Molly Peacock

Kentucky Swami by Tim Skeen, selected by Michael Burns

The Resurrection Machine by Steve Gehrke, selected by Miller Williams